Called Back

Called Back

Rosa Lane

Tupelo Press
North Adams, MA

ISBN-13: 978-1-961209-10-7
Library of Congress Control Number: 2024933497

Design by Allison O'Keefe

Cover Art: "Opening" by Joan Fullerton. Mixed media collage. Private collection. Used by permission of the artist.

First paperback edition September 2024.

Tupelo Press
P.O. Box 1767
North Adams, Massachusetts 01247
(413) 664-9611 / Fax: (413) 664-9711
editor@tupelopress.org / www.tupelopress.org

Tupelo Press is an award-winning independent literary press that publishes fine fiction, non-fiction, and poetry in books that are a joy to hold as well as read. Tupelo Press is a registered 501(c)(3) non-profit organization, and we rely on public support to carry out our mission of publishing extraordinary work that may be outside the realm of the large commercial publishers. Financial donations are welcome and are tax deductible.

THE POEMS OF EMILY DICKINSON, edited by Thomas H. Johnson, Cambridge, Mass.: The Belknap Press of Harvard University Press, Copyright © 1951, 1955 by the President and Fellows of Harvard College. Copyright © renewed 1979, 1983 by the President and Fellows of Harvard College. Copyright © 1914, 1918, 1919, 1924, 1929, 1930, 1932, 1935, 1937, 1942, by Martha Dickinson Bianchi. Copyright © 1952, 1957, 1958, 1963, 1965, by Mary L. Hampson. Used by permission. All rights reserved.

THE LETTERS OF EMILY DICKINSON, edited by Thomas H. Johnson, Associate Editor, Theodora Ward, Cambridge, Mass.: The Belknap Press of Harvard University Press, Copyright © 1958 by the President and Fellows of Harvard College. Copyright © renewed 1986 by the President and Fellows of Harvard College. Copyright © 1914, 1924, 1932, 1942 by Martha Dickinson Bianchi. Copyright © 1952 by Alfred Leete Hampson. Copyright © 1960 by Mary L. Hampson. Used by permission. All rights reserved.

This project is supported in part by an award from the National Endowment for the Arts

for the othered

Most — I love the Cause that slew Me.

—Emily Dickinson (925, line 17)

Contents

I.

Othered [I speak]

Her breast is fit for pearls,
But I was not a 'Diver' —
Her brow is fit for thrones
But I have not a crest.
　　　　　　—Emily Dickinson (84, lines 1-4)

I am wrong to start with,
　　　　to have //

to strop & hone the blade,
　　　　shave without a tuft //

to bind, bone-wrap my breasts,
　　　　they will not leave //

to swag my trousers & waistcoat
　　　　in a dark no one sees //

to ramrod the barrel, gun-cock, lean
　　　　a corner, the house dead-ends //

to hike sails, captain my ship, doldrumed
　　　　drifting nowhere windless //

to bypass the lungs, drop my voice
　　　　to the diaphragm, timbre gravitas //

to smoke my meerschaum, virile & fragrant
　　　　blending Latakia, smoke rings in solo //

I kerf the flesh of Adam's apple verboten, pith
　　　　the larynx, my mouth plosive — hushed //　·

For Eve at the Evergreens

> *The Martyr Poets — did not tell —*
> *But wrought their Pang in syllable —*
>   —Emily Dickinson (544, lines 1-2)

On the brink of spilling
        everything, tines swell

        & bead. I tap
the well's rim, pinch my dip-

pen's throat, nib-scratch manilla. Iron gall
        ink, each excess rocker-

        blotted. I bleed
another black cloud, backlit

by lambent light. My sheet
        grows an orchard

        where you graze. I hunt
your cloven path by way of lava heat

fevered in that trough between couplets
        our breasts pique

        ash — choking Vesuvian.
Our sapphic love disallowed

by blueprint. You dissever. I belly-lock
        & refuse to pass

the key to the inevitable buck
browsing our hungry fence

at dusk. Indelible, I marry my writing
table, give it my whole hand.

The Victorian Dissident

I had been hungry, all the Years —
My Noon had Come — to dine —
            —Emily Dickinson (579, lines 1-2)

Ruffians rattle
        loose winter's cusp
                & gust the Evergreens —
                birches shiver   silver

bent cold. William IV sterling
        unseats its velvet
                box, your Victorian
                mahogany

set for twelve. My hunger behaves
        your table, I starve
                my demons. Feral
                utterances take oath

to quash. Of course, I slip back
        into my corner nook
                of the Homestead —
                the 4-square lantern lit,

its mustard circle, folio,
        a locket of your hair,
                my red cedar
                graphite. Gray geometries

of my chair lattice
       the wall & oscillate. I undo
          every symmetry
          & by twilight, I poof

my breath across the glass chimney,
       snuff kerosene
          light. Again, my dawn
          wakes ruby — I rebel & dissent.

French Sardines

Wild Nights — Wild Nights!
Were I with thee
Wild Nights should be
Our luxury!
          —Emily Dickinson (249, lines 1-4)

        French sardines arrive from Boston, tin-
plated. Maggie levers her can
                    cutter

at the edge, jacks her hand around the lid
      of hunger's fulcrum. Silver-
                    skinned

      and nested, their caudal fins swim a sea
of marinade — white salt cured,
                    drenched

in extra virgin. Beheaded & gutted
      by the women of Nantes,
                    we lay

      each body across a soda cracker I have
for days dreamed of. Craving.
                    Nights

behind each pearly eye, we swim
      up the fish weir, we
                    spawn

in sandy silt along the odic
thighs of the Loire, we flutter
                    our little deaths.

Gentian

After Emily Dickinson's
"I taste a liquor never brewed —" (214)

To own a Susan of my own
Is of itself a Bliss —
Whatever Realm I forfeit, Lord,
Continue me in this!
          —Emily Dickinson (1401)

Near the washbasin, I snip locks
          of red laid

          on the commode. I strip
your shoulder bare, unbutton

your back, pearl by pearl
          down the arch, hands as silken

          as our path, grass-worn — its spine
stretching your Evergreens

to my Homestead. Sateen lace-ups
          in step — breasts intoxicated

          with letters we exchange
at the hedge, each pressed

with gentian, trumpets or bitters,
          or the drunken tonic

of King Gentius. Call me his
prince — below the crown, my forehead

flattens against the pane, framed
        in a glaze. When our lit chambers

        face, we watch the sun drop
evenings behind the steeple,

hangover Amherst woods whisking
        dark, stagger

        nightfall — bliss-blued drunk.

Foxglove [disambiguation]

When 'Landlords' turn the drunken Bee
Out of the Foxglove's door —
         —Emily Dickinson (214, lines 9-10)

I have been fooled
      by freckled
   foxglove before, taken
   residence —
      sipped her magenta shades. She
filled my stein, *Tippler* tricked
   yet again. Evicted.

     ﹏

In van Gogh's *yellow period*, he ate
      a glove, they said —
   blue halo
   hazing each sharp point
      of light nipping his meadow,
all else faded young squash.

     ﹏

In 1542, Fuchs recorded the first fox-
      glove, his German surname
   meant *fox*. And Latin for finger,
   digitalis. In groups of five,
      a glove, or on each finger a cot
fitted to the first knuckle.

Foxes Glofe, Old English
   witch's weed — whipping maelstrom,
  those thimbles of trouble — noxious remedy
  full mooned, or the troubadour's mirage,
   a ballad's bribe — floral spirits
airborne at the stream.

Foxes gloved their paws —
   slipshoed,
  crept fabled hunts, silenced
  their crouch to prey —
   dens dinting medieval fields.

Popping the fence, a ladder
   of these apartments, innocent
  as baby teeth socketing a green jaw
  in July — bare-
   breasted, flared skirt
waist-gathered, swinging

a serpent tail, bearded
        wattles, flaunt
      her curled rim doorways. I bend
      to lip love
        and pollenate. And each time I suck
from that empty space

where the horn blows
        out her cheeks
      selling vacancy, feint —
      admitted, I glut amrita,
        gorge her tubes
of god. I swill — a vagrant lit at each revolving door.

Dear Sir,
(No. 1)

Just Infinites of Nought —
As far as it could see —
                    –Emily Dickinson (458, lines 5-6)

Windows act cruel today // No zephyr
or tapering // Eve basks the orchard //

My sparrow tucks into her breasted swale /
that holy crevice / or hell's cleft

between hills torn from an atlas /
the abyss / their rift hovers // The unruly

little beak tells her to pirate
the sweetest Rome / divine the reptant tail //

She comes with scent from her tuft /
tortures me with musk / fresh peach

and salmon // A turkey vulture surveils
overhead / the preacher's monocle / scanning

for deviants all day // Caught / in headwinds
I catch my plunge from the cock-

loft / teeter cracks between floorboards /
tightrope the attic / my country

seized // I expunge a nervous night /
a refugee already weary from a future

grieved / obsessed / unlived — taken

Dear Sir,
(No. 4)

Society for me my misery
Since Gift of Thee —
  —Emily Dickinson (1534)

Vortex of heart, or

  lone star fixed — barred coupling. I

    dissent, burn a scream

  my love of her — doomed, sapphic,

disobedient. Damned shut!

Sparrow's Sonnet

'Hope' is the thing with feathers —
    —Emily Dickinson (254, line 1)

Hope is a subtle Glutton —
    —Emily Dickinson (1547, line 1)

Sparrow / Egyptian's *little bad* // Soul catcher // Or
perhaps a seadog's tattoo swooping the drowned
into paradise // Or Sappho's winged team *pulling*
Aphrodite's chariot // Or symbol of Festus's
lewd antics of man's hideous part // I adopt instead
Catullus and his Lesbia's beloved pet *in sinu* tucked
into her cleavage / that feathered heart suckling
her finger // Lavish gives way to the irritated
nip / I know / yet follows the portending peck
of love and the forgiven nose / that human neb buried
inside cheek-soft burnished gray // I wait chariot-ready //
My sparrow sweeps your second story // See my beaded
eye / my breast wing *hope* / you dismiss // I unplume
your balsam / leave my flight on your sill / bound

Dear Sir,
(No. 7)

> *And They no more remember me —*
> *Nor ever turn to tell me why —*
> *Oh, Master, This is Misery —*
> > —Emily Dickinson (462, lines 11-3)

> *Love's stricken 'why'*
> *Is all that love can speak —*
> > —Emily Dickinson (1368, lines 1-2)

Tell me, Sir, why I wake
with a bird in my mouth.

Why my heart seeks
a nest in a sparrow's beak
when I worship want
on the tip of her wing.

Why when I visit Eden,
I want Eve, not Adam.

Why I long for doors
that cannot open.

Why I plant myself
in situ, move about light, yet
cannot lift my feet.

Why I live
more myth than element.

Why I fold myself
in a letter delivered elsewhere,
my address unopened
still lying on the table.

Why my finger inserts
the loop of a hot teacup
its curved lip sips, kisses
a future not yet.

Why the moon comes
to my window full bellied,
stares — *why*
when I reach for her, she empties,
turns sickle, leaves me
in shreds.

My Voyage

Mediterranean intonations —
To a Current's Ear —
There is a maritime conviction
In the Atmosphere —
                    —Emily Dickinson (1302, lines 5-8)

Each night I curl inside my ink well, set afloat
my alabaster kingdom & tack my way

to Egypt. I find you past the Mediterranean
grove — its breath shifting cedars, the Nile

undulating a path to the barn. I return to Rome
under the bower — apple blossoms, a spray

of lupines, their cups spike lapis shades, open-
mouthed, cascades of a love catcher's crave —

Gray misting cold waters, I watch your zest
sail another's horizon, flip back your Arabian hair.

Dear Susan, I am your Antony — Emily D.

> *'Egypt — thou knew'st'* —
> > –from Dickinson's letter (L 430) sent to Susan
> > Huntington Dickinson (about 1874) quoting
> > Shakespeare's *Antony and Cleopatra*
> > (Antony, III, xi, 60)

Wind-driven, I'm off

    to Alexandria, torqued,

        compassed *mare nostrum* —

    keel, ribs, tongues' hardwood, cockled

beguiled, you sway me steady.

Marooned

The difference between Despair
And Fear — is like the One
Between the instant of a Wreck —
And when the Wreck has been —
                  —Emily Dickinson (305, lines 1-4)

Counterweighted, my upper sash
    blurs sunrise under-

    water — magenta's wavy ribbon
bleeds southeast. Our planked road

laden muddy stars dew-wet
    silica. I trace

    bubbles of artisan's breath
glinting glass —

blaze dawn's tinder, brimstone-
    tipped. Gritty eyed

    I abandon the mud hook. Any minute
Maggie will knock with morning tea,

freshen damp linen, remove
    the chamber pot.

    My windows rotate the day
south, then twist west. Inside eve,

I find you in the bedchamber
        fringed in balsam. When you lie

        at the edge of my brother,
I strike the sky with a match —

light a star I follow, float the dark
        to your upper sash, wash up wrecked.

My Cleopatra

Should a shrewd betray me —
Atropos decide!
                    —Emily Dickinson (11, lines 20-1)

Belled blooms / inky pome

    Atropa belladonna

      named for *Atropos* /

    Third Fate // You drink her herb / reck-

less / gift our live threads / she cuts

In the bedlam of my chest

Snow beneath whose chilly softness
Some that never lay
Make their first Repose this Winter
I admonish Thee
                    —Emily Dickinson (942, lines 1-4)

I mount my roan   unbridled
          ride sorrel woods   under December

oaks   a few puce leaves still refuse
          October's fall   morocco and crisp   rattle

their solitary fits   I ride trail-frozen into an asylum
          of snow at the outskirt of town

where last week the nor'easter imposed
          her commons   Pastures graze arm-in-arm

Fences lower their rails   Roofs
          blanket under the same sweep

inseparable   Even chimneys cluster their kitchens
          smoking ash   curling night air

crackling a soft boil   Tonight   I left you
          behind shivery glass   Candles

darken their wicks   Your titian window
          disappearing light   I see your face frost

every pane I pass   Frigid winds
          whip corners to the brink   whistle me mad

Kiting April —

A Pang is more conspicuous in Spring
In contrast with the things that sing
Not Birds entirely — but Minds —
Minute Effulgencies and Winds —
          —Emily Dickinson (1530, lines 1-4)

find me in white — billowing
south wind, flat chest

shaped by darts. Inside my pocket,
a poem folded on the back

of an envelope teases my pencil. I push
the breast-plow — garden thawed

third week. Crocuses already blooming
centuries ahead. I till and turn

the bed, soak my seasonal brain
like seed. Mud-kneed. I edge and furrow —

winter forgiven. I reach for the jar,
pour the whole garden into my apron-

draped bowl. And where frost left
its wound, I drop a seed

into the *o* of pock — a soft vowel
planted between consonants. Beware

the clicking jaws of the aphid-
mind. And how the emerald march

of these tiny dots can skive
a whole plot. And when sheaths crack

open their specters, shoot up
esophagi, unfurl their mouths for cupping

copper blue, the poem will unfold
its envelope, release every pinion, slant

upward full timbre, skirr the empyrean.

Poiesis

Depths of Ruby, undrained,
Hid, Lip, for Thee ——
Play it were a Humming Bird ——
And just sipped —— me ——
                —Emily Dickinson (334, lines 5-8)

Ruby throats unzip
the page
            recto holds
            a steed clamped
            between legs

        entering Celtic woods
bareback,
            damp smell
            of Scottish fern,
            spills fresh teen

        hymen-red
touch-me-nots
            rush wings
            across the meadow
            of little deaths ——

        This is how
the throated
            ruby descends
            the verso —— syllabic
            speed, fifty-three beats

per second, she sips
my impatiens, rouged
  in secret, full-
  lipped, the pod explodes —
  repels the gravity she succumbs

II.

Arabian Nights, #1

Like Eyes that looked on Wastes —
Incredulous of Ought
      —Emily Dickinson (458, lines 1-2)

Maggie roams the belly — stove to dry sink,
flour barrel to salted fish hung by hook in the pantry.

I drop little words of love into slots. Pull my chair
into dinner's envelope   taut to table set — code speak

hunger. Moon captured by upper pane, my head
drops notches to hold her rising — she floods the glass.

Little gods armed with oughts, I betray. Unravel
my white linen robe, naked by kerosene, wicking.

My journey rows down the hall, wall-braced
each dipped oar. I drown on father's ziggurat of stairs.

A hound howls passed midnight. I tack next life,
unhurt *the bearded Pronoun* she, curry my wooly chin.

Dear Divers, *my Fellow Men* —

> *Take all away from me, but leave me Ecstasy,*
> *And I am richer then than all my Fellow Men* —
> — Emily Dickinson (1640, lines 1-2)

> *Did the 'Paradise' — persuaded —*
> *Yield her moat of pearl —*
> *Would the Eden be an Eden,*
> *Or the Earl — an Earl?*
> — Emily Dickinson (213, lines 5-8)

Eden laps my pillow —
              without lodestars
      or rhumb, I row

your wake into the lee's
              chop, moor
      and high dive

the quilt, my whole tabernacle
              under tented knees.
      Inside Leyda's

omitted center I lie — the marine
              rondure for reckless nights
      diving *pearl*. Not you, Divers,

but I, her bearded bride-
              groom, roll that *pearl*
      between fingers, take

my ungiven right of way. The boy
        of me riddled inside
    Eden. Your bounty

hunters case the wrong field. Come
        to my phantom
    mead. I am here

in Sappho's asphodels. See me?
        Leontodon standing
    there, the *Earl*

ruling on one tubular leg, my puffed
        cowl aged white,
    ready to blow my pistil and seed.

Dents de Lion

Pappus, a clock
　　　　of seed,
　　full halo

　　　　　　lunar puff. My parachute
　　　a host
of soft bristles
　　　　ferries me
　　miles

　　　　　　from my single parent
　　wind-
blown. Metrical
　　　　feet scale
　　fragments

　　　　　　in the daily pocket
　　　of my garden
dress, summer's
　　　　hands
　　sweet

　　　　　　　with dirt. Each fascicle
　　　　　a bundle
of vibrissae
　　　　　suspended
　　　by vortex

　　　　　　that eddy
　　　　of air, my bristled
tailwind lands
　　　　　my descent
　　　to the common

　　　　　　meadow, or
　　　　to the sandy mortar
between walkway stones.
　　　I am
　　　the golden medallion

　　　　　　sun stippling
　　　　earth, I feather
my plume,
　　　　leafy toothed
　　　grown basil,

　　　　　　my serrated dents
　　　　de lion —
immortal, *called back*
　　　　relentless, I roar —
　　　madden every single plot.

The Daguerreotype [camera obscura]

Frozen ninety seconds, I staged
          the pretended
      parlor. Propped. The book. Dead
flowers in hand, as if

I just returned from Homestead's
          garden fecund. As if
      before the vase,
I stopped shy

of the kitchen,
          slipped off my head
      scarf, slid into the slat
back, leaned the table

pinned on an elbow
          perhaps to muse
      the closed book. My guise
captured on a sixth plate, fixed

barren and bootless,
          that copper substrate,
      silver-washed
fuming iodine. Father's favor

immortalized, airtight
          framed lifeless — God
      forbid my edges
might breathe, darken

his mantle with no quick or rash,
                 nor eyes their hazel. Shot
      by a salesman
he paid — miniature seized

on a latent leaf. I stared into the box —
             its black hole brass-
      ringed, he slid me into
his eye, held me

in a trigger. And when his umbrella puffed
             its limelight, I
      left my body
in the chair, my elbow still resting on the table.

Arabian Nights, #2

A Life quite ready to depart
Can harass me no more —
　　　　　　—Emily Dickinson (858, lines 19-20)

Father demanded the daguerreotype for token
proof / copperplate mirror shined / rosed in iodine /

toned gold // My non-face suffocates // Sexless
wind / genderless wind // Know I lift your skirt

from a shy love // Yes, I am callow // I am
the bearded Pronoun unknown as she // Windows

cataract overnight / morning rimed // Maggie
hangs out our bedclothes / clipped and cambric /

slatting air // At my death's anniversary / you reveled
lush / lavish / drunk // My Cleopatra / I am

your Antony // I admit only by quixotic mind did I
follow your gest / battle / lose your whole country

Susan's Calls are like Antony's Supper —

Susan's Calls are like Antony's Supper —
'And pays his Heart for what his Eyes eat, only —'
        –from Dickinson's letter (L 854) sent to
        Susan Huntington Dickinson (spring 1883)
        with quote from Shakespeare's *Antony and*
        Cleopatra (Enobarbus, II, ii, 264-5)

Here at the edge
of the Mediterranean, I behold
your Egypt. You strut
my sword Philippan
and swipe. I in your linen
sheath, my head queened
bound by diadem.

Last week, I fought your war, my army
charged Arabian dunes, buried
by mirage. Still, I chase
your lizard into the attic,
that jeweled chameleon, more exquisite
each season's turn.

I shovel coal into the bucket, shiny
shards luster. Father's sitting room
radiates heavy heat. Carboned.
Wood smoke from Maggie's kitchen
wind-swoops dinner, you
join. *My eyes*
feast, the heart's famish. You cock
your crowned palate
and spurn. I swallow back
my sword.

Paire de corps

Amputate my freckled Bosom!
Make me bearded like a man!
        —Emily Dickinson (1737, lines 3-4)

Paire de corps, a pair of bodies hangs
from my chest, sistered and whale-boned

in a cuff. I want nothing of them. Still,
tethered and corseted, these oddments, small

thimbles, two berries made for the mouth,
speak a primal language not mine. A wolf's

ravish. Or the infant's
pucker for milk, a utensil gorged

and sucked. Those fleshy hills are there
for swallowing. Wan, two drifts of snow,

windblown, renounced. Razed
by slice or tear, my bust blanked.

My sternum flanked by ribs, basal flat
[   ] [   ] like paired caesuras. Phantom

nipples hover endless pause. My hairless
chin densed and wild, my mouth

squared. I am my beard, edged
along the jaw — tinted curls free-

fall, re-pronouned — plumed and prow.

Clothesline

      Our nightclothes
    whip the line, clipped
side by side, swell

      & billow frantic
   for embodiment. Cold
winds advantage our absence,

     inflate,
   take up habitation
throughout the day — makeshift

     pro tempore. Can you see
  our vacancies weave
& twist our arms

     flailing? Our night
  clothes crawl the afternoon —
elongate shadows. We

     slither the barn-
  yard's first frost, crust
last summer's grass.

     Peeking green
  escape, see

how we play dead,

        emptiness

    slat dry, huffs

hung back

        into our Cimmerian closet

   replete.

Feral nights curl

'Twas warm — at first — like Us —
Until there crept upon
A Chill — like frost upon a Glass —
Till all the scene — be gone.
                    —Emily Dickinson (519, lines 1-4)

    dawn at the foot   purr legs
of the breakfast table   switch

    a tail end-hook   acute   ears swivel
my watch   for your skirt skimming late

    October's crystalline path   I see you
at a distance   I exhaust the morning

    windows   sleep to the witching
hour   Noon's desire

    mounting   a rood
decoupling

    and the inevitable
decline into late afternoon

    creeping raw dusk   Our lit windows
match gold, quaver

    Eve's gelid grove   Above
all of Amherst   you allow me

a glimpse of your silhouette
my cat eye at the second story

Your waist flickering
candlelight   hands bedim   buried in fur

my forehead heats
a hole in the breath-

ferned   whiskered opalescent glass

My Windows

By my Window have I for Scenery
Just a Sea — with a Stem —
                    —Emily Dickinson (797, lines 1-2)

My windows listen. I inhale their faces, touch
        their tones.

My windows excite April. Sparrows circus,
acrobat straw
        after straw.

My west window breaks a bird's neck —
thumps a feather stuck
        to the middle pane.

My windows drain winter light. I light a candle,
exhale diamonds and melt
        my face.

My windows portal the sea, I master waves —
bed to commode, commode to wardrobe,
wardrobe to bureau, bureau back to my shifted
        seabed.

My windows smoke fog, smolder spring
meadows —
        burning off the brume.

My windows roast my room, turn a spit
in slow smelt. I hoist iron weighted in the jamb —
        lift the air.

All day my windows slide cages around the room,
slanting parallels. I climb between mullions
        into the far wall.

My windows rope and pulley my body
fixed on a sea-
        cliff.

My windows wear me thin.

My windows gift me lapis mornings,
inky nights —
        pearled obsidian.

My windows peel thunder, clap
the wall
        in a bolt.

I make my windows talk, tap syllables, replace
        my blind eye.

I carry my windows in my pocket
· what their eyes
        have seen.

Jasminum

Double-edged, crickets
      scissor, electrify evening. I linger
         the porch

after dinner. Intoxicated, jasmine's
      ambrosial spray pinwheels
         and drapes the lattice.

Dusk releases *Poet's Jasmine*
      in its Persian summer,
         Queen of the Night —

like Cleopatra's sails soaked
      in *yasmin* oils
         infused Ionian breezes

to lure. The exotic *White Arabian*
      and her sensual climb
         animalic. You

do not know I poured
      us tea. You do not know the breath
         of *Ninlil* brought you

here. How nightfall weeps musk,
      tenders the missing. I snip
         your scent and sip.

Far Reach

A galaxy between us
        I hold
                its compressed burn
Your nightstand's wicked light

nettles midnight ruthless
        navy
                years of it
My solo speck stretches the arbor

a whole chest of fire
        · hexed
                with the ambered fever
of bees   honeycombed   I admit

my window extends
        telescopic
                Runic hours
propel my beeline's

arrival inside
        your scarlet whorl
                my apis hum vibrating
gold to the inside leg Please

forgive my figment's vector
    · of love Unmet
          I fluff my rear bristles
in diapause   shiver out the cold

Arcturus

'Arcturus' is his other name —
I'd rather call him 'Star.'
       —Emily Dickinson (70, lines 1-2)

Red orange pinpoint —
pricks the Big Dipper's

handle. Thirty-seven years
of travel for this

tiny firethorn to april
my Homestead, bring my helve

to harrow. At the equinox
this noisy plowman

drives oxen yelling his hungry
dogs around the poles

Canes Venatici, or hunting for *Enlil*,
god of the gardener, inventor

of hoe. Every spring we meet
between heaven and earth, plant

that seam — ribs of beets and beans,
a hedge of roses, figs, lilacs, sweet

Williams — clamorous scents
in spectra of light, my metronome

of sky. Tribute. My old *Star* grows
riotous, colder — I know

one day he will carry me back. We
will dim, surrender the dogs,

store his carriage, bereave our field
gone fallow, and for the last time

hang *Enlil's* hoe on the barn wall.

III.

Last Fall

'Tis true — *They shut me in the Cold* —
               –Emily Dickinson (538, line 1)

I smell fence like a fox, our common meadow
outbound, more feudal now. I travel my bed —

dream of our love   you cordon cold. The hound
tethered to my side, I spoon his hunt yipping

prey, headboard to foot. Death stops, smells
the fence, divines and crosses the hyssop. Now

my compass — the fever's bearing, waist
in agony. Tonight, sunset bleeds a mottled rash,

my walls rust   rotted Romes. Tinctured, I deign —
harvest nothing. Where you vanish so I die, unborn.

Today, I go fugitive —

After Emily Dickinson's
"It was not Death, for I stood up," (510)

lay low & slither dog, nose trail for ruins, signs
of decay — fruit, rust-speckled, aging Eden exotic,

sepia-toned. I walk the Mediterranean summer spooling
down death's drum — Eve's cadence. Each beat I roll

spindle sticks, bloom-ended, tempo-wristed, tap. Laminar
veils, vermillion, saffron, cobalt — illuminate a wall

just as a poet's mother saw light & pointed hours before
her flight fissures Arabian dusk. This is how we go.

Chroma zigzagging drumfire overhead. I brush off
the desert, unfurl the umbrella, summon my way back.

Dear Sir,
(No. 3)

After Emily Dickinson's
"As Summer into Autumn slips" (1346)

Last of the Canada geese forms and frets,
spearheads south, their honking yodels

curdle and break Amherst's blue hour.
The north has come to get us

early. Crows lout, aggravate
their thievery pecking

harvest remains. Maggie pushes the hen
onto the spit for supper, boils

summer's epilogue, the cookstove's crack
and pop. Bessie's feathers clotted

beside the fresh stump, her spirit feet
still puffed, hacked at the hock joint,

strut her sacrifice into another world, I
succumb to eat. Today, I recover

from the attic my black cape, its urgency
hooked, keen-eyed. I know the wind

grows near lunacy for the loose. My bulbs
will freeze, dream life below zero. I

comfort before the fire, chasten
my future. And Sir, despite slow depletion

of winter's stash, I promise to minister
a brave hunger. No matter survival

or death — for you, I foment
spring's earliest   bloodred bloom.

Bedchamber, Last Days

> *Because I could not stop for Death —*
> *He kindly stopped for me —*
>   —Emily Dickinson (712, lines 1-2)

In and out of the sleigh bed, my feet agitate, scuff
small ovals into the floor. Up again, my white night

gown sweeps the west window to the east and back.
I see you from the Homestead — your bedchamber

grates the eve. Ghosting, you close the curtains, trans-
lucent, and torment. I hold the mantle above midnight

fire, steady the fainting brain, my face
swells. The cough will not let up — no sleep.

I scribble my desk. My herbarium tangles
and untangles vines and flora. I walk my wallpaper,

slip you into Maggie's trunk, fragments
she knows to burn when death's sol rises ashen

that day, and beyond the stellar ambit *He* takes me.

Bedchamber with Bright's

After Emily Dickinson's
"There is a pain — so utter —" (599)

Late afternoon — wet sun after rain,
auric rays on a misty rake. Maggie knocks,

brings a tray of biscuits, cozied teapot,
teacup with handle, amphibious. I count

wallpapered leaves on the vine, climb
the trellis to the crown chamfered

and beveled. Below the leaves, crickets
serrate nightfall, fireflies flick dust by oil

light, stream my ceiling, a galaxy. The wall
cracks a ziggurat, quaking. I spill in bed

tinted ruby. I wait in the slat back for Maggie
to change sheets, glass shards in my belly. She

washes me again. I walk the arbor, pluck
the peduncles — eat every grape as I go.

Limning, Death

I felt a Funeral, in my Brain,
      —Emily Dickinson (280, line 1)

She dealt her pretty words like Blades —
      —Emily Dickinson (479, line 1)

Immortalities strut around this Homestead as if they own
everything, their ceremonial stop at the mantle — forevering.

Father's daguerreotypes seal our faces — brass-matted,
muted, red velvet softens a haze of black bleeding in.

My little room more shadow than light spins on the wheel
of death. I am an impalement artist — one knife toss away

from the thrower's mistake. I disappear in tiny mouthfuls
each day. I study any sign of being taken, my room

stunned by morning, I am still here. Yesterday, I died again —
swept myself into a dustpan, rattled the windows

like a beggar's cup. I yearn for the perennial garden, yet I
have no gender. Just the moon waxing her want at the bluff.

Transitus, when the blue mist rises

You cannot fold a Flood —
And put it in a Drawer —
      —Emily Dickinson (530, lines 5-6)

I hover. Only my body
     inhabits space,

a deserted village
     you trespass —

you bathe
     my streets, snuff gas

lamps yellowing
     the common. You

close my lids, clip cowlicks —
     understories

overgrowing the banks
     of Fort River. I lean into

the field's
     narrow neck, you

unwrap the bandage,
     kiss the wound, rosed

by yet another
     May — I smell coming. You

turn your back as if
        you could ignore

the river ascending
        its limbic rim, rushing

past my bureau, my bed
        already carried down

rapids. Our secret purpling
        hyacinths in a vase of regret.

I descend the stairs
        in a box balanced

on the shoulders
        of six Irishmen.

Vinnie's violets
        dress my throat,

the back door open
        to my garden. I lie

in the parlor —
        two heliotropes

in hand, blood-
        stones, earthy green

flecked with Jasper —
    its bright red reminder

before redemption,
    before nyctinastic

close, wounds lay bare
    in evenfall's last light.

Dear Sir,
(No. 6)

After Emily Dickinson's
"After a hundred years" (1147)

Since then — 'tis Centuries — and yet
Feels shorter than the Day
I first surmised the Horses' Heads
Were toward Eternity —
                    —Emily Dickinson (712, lines 21-4)

My bones lay in a bed
of dust, jangle the stygian

box. The depressed whorl
of earth at the soft pock

behind my headstone. My breasts
disappear in cones of dreck

I sweep. My beard
still thickens. My hair

a river of red
extends my waist. I swim

the meadow, collect stars
in a basket. I see

light echo shade
where my horses whisper

and blink a universe,
I live. My sparrows wing

ahead with no care
for the blues left

in their tailwinds. I strum
my ribs full octave

like a barbiton lyre
for the Dionysians. I chant

canticles. My lungs
breathe pink as tulips. I sail

the Ionian Sea, drift
the lilacs. My arms unspool

rings of the tallest pine. My hoofs
trot the dark, canter

Puffer's edge. I
listen for syllables, pause

every dash. Oh Sir,
if you could have had me

outlive a century, I
would have known you

as tutelary wave. Your holograms
radiating my blooms, patterns of you

cohering fragrance
in wavy light. The Homestead

and the Evergreens crisscrossing
serpentine paths, never the same

trajectory or loop — that strange
attractor — I now know as good.

IV.

The *Loaded Gun* (Translation No. 1)

After Emily Dickinson's
"My Life had stood — a Loaded Gun —" (754)

The name They dropped upon my face
With water, in the country church
Is finished using, now,
                —Emily Dickinson (508, lines 2-4)

Caving for years, I dug
the mine for peter

dirt, flooded, blending
wood ash — remnants

of fire, crystalized —
flaring saltpeter, a fuse

of sulfur & carbon. I
lay a black line

on paper, roll a tube
of war, twisted

ends, death — spark
& powder. I fill the pan,

ramrod the silken shot
down the barrel's hole, I

cannot muster. The rack
cradles the impotent

gun, undying
powder resting in a horn,

its spring-loaded mouth
capped like the preacher's loch

plugged with the Rose,
a name, I was not. My head

sprinkled three times for a father,
son & holy ghost, I left

the Rose in a pew. Name-
less until that day I passed

the mirror, saw a boy I knew
was I, self-same, twinned aberrant.

⁓

Riding shotgun, my gun
belongs to the fawn's leap

across the firth's looking
glass. I am the hunted. Caught

in the cross-
hairs, I stand at the perch

& cock for the quidnunc's
fooled beliefs   comply —

I defy. I am a prisoner of war,
lay my spots on the road, jocund

for the cause — my face
renamed, so august.

The *Loaded Gun* (Translation No. 2)

After Emily Dickinson's
"My Life had stood — a Loaded Gun —" (754)

I felt a Cleaving in my Mind —
As if my Brain had split —
        —Emily Dickinson (937, lines 1-2)

My halfness tended the orphaned
thing, loaded the flint-
      lock, its quotidian

desire for powder,
to ram — her thumb
      docile. The gun

mounting charge, endlessly
latent, disowned.
      My halfness minted

a nickel's one-sided
Indian head
      or Lady Liberty's half-

dime, pursed & paltry
until Power passed —
      recognized his lock-

plate, nipple & hammer. He
gave me his beard. Espied,
      he made me

half-stag, whole. My voice
skates the pond —
        registers bass, echoing

a deep mettle. My days peak
your Evergreens, I rut & track
        your cloven path

my nights crown. I
lie in my beard
        more pouf than down,

I rifle
othering. & if
        in a rift, my beard

effaced, I will coffin, lock
my horns, strike
        back the fuse I come from.

The *Loaded Gun* (Translation No. 3)

After Emily Dickinson's
"My Life had stood — a Loaded Gun —" (754)

I'm ceded — I've stopped being Theirs —
—Emily Dickinson (508, line 1)

I knew the *loaded gun* / stood / for the non-
belonging // When ten / I studied weapons

of medieval war // carved in a shed /
lit by oil // One thing /

certain / my knife was urgent // whittling
the precise eye / along the grain /

smoothed by grit / the silken edge
of a dagger / battle-ready /

my sword / its decorative pommel / the grip
wrapped with a tongue

from an old boot // the cruciform
hilt // blade hewn to fatal point

swaggering my hip // crossbow and arrows
slung my back // You see / I loved

the butcher's daughter // but she married / the boy
with my cousin's name // who knew

he was the boy / I wanted / to be //
I made three cases full //

buried them / hatches / hinged
flush / with woods

soil // Please know / it is not
so much / I did this //

but the unquestionable
necessity of it / the child's battle

cry in the woods / fearless /
valiant / her young dissent /

her willingness *to die / for the rebel to live*

NOTES

Called Back, the title of this collection, are the last two words Emily Dickinson wrote in a letter to her Norcross cousins before her death. Dickinson was referencing *Called Back*, the title of Hugh Conway's novel (Bristol: J. W. Arrowsmith) first published in 1883. These two words, *Called Back*, are also engraved on Dickinson's headstone, which this collection borrows as its title.

Selections from Dickinson's poems are taken from Thomas H. Johnson's (ed.) *The Complete Poems of Emily Dickinson* (New York: Back Bay Books / Little, Brown and Company, 1976) and are used with permission from Harvard University Press.

Selections from Dickinson's letters are taken from Thomas H. Johnson (ed.) and Theodora Ward's (assoc. ed.) *The Letters of Emily Dickinson* (Cambridge: The Belknap Press of Harvard University Press, 1958, 1986) and are used with permission from Harvard University Press.

This author primarily utilizes the word "Sir" in place of the word "Master," except in this collection where the word is defined within the text itself. Indeed, the word "Master" is known to have several meanings, usages, and references; however, its meaning by which this word is or was used to identify white male entitlement in socio-historical relations of enslavement, ownership of enslaved persons, and inhuman treatment casts an unwelcome shadow upon this word. Though Dickinson did not use the word in promoting such horrific meaning, she titled a person/ entity as "Master" in selected poems and in her *Master Letters*. In her *Master Letters*, Dickinson identifies "Master" as a bearded man, whom she imbued with knowledge, empowerment, and agency. In her work, Dickinson also addresses this person/entity as "Sir," which this collection uses.

Following Judith Farr in her work, *The Passion of Emily Dickinson* (Cambridge: Harvard University Press, 1992), certain poems within this collection utilize various code or pet names by which Dickinson referred to Susan Huntington (Gilbert) Dickinson including: bird, bumblebee, Cleopatra, Dollie, Eden, eternity, Eve, heaven, jewel, lily, pearl, rose, sunset, and Vesuvius among others. Farr also proposes Dickinson's use of the word "Diver" in poem 84 refers to "*man*" (p. 134), who is privileged by gender to dive for "pearls."

In "Dear Sir, (No. 1)" and in "The Last Fall," the word "Rome" in both poems refers to a type of apple with its origin dating back to the early 1800s when it grew from an "accidental" seedling in Rome Township, Ohio.

"Sparrow's Sonnet" references several meanings and italicized words and phrases borrowed from Alexander Lee's essay, "Catullus and Lesbia's Sparrow" (*History Today*, Volume 71, Issue 5, May 2021): https://www.historytoday.com/archive/natural-histories/catullus-and-lesbias-sparrow

"Dear Sir, (No. 7)" is both a "letter-poem" and a "list poem," which in consecutive stanzas repeats anaphorically the word "Why" as used in Dickinson's epigraphs that inspired this poem. The phrase "letter-poem" was first used by Susan Huntington Dickinson in 1891 to describe the genre of Dickinson's letters, which were written with short lines as referenced in Ellen Louise Hart and Martha Nell Smith's (eds.) *Open Me Carefully* (Middletown, CT: Wesleyan Press, 2019, 1st published by Paris Press, 1998).

In "Dear Susan, I am your Antony — Emily D.," the epigraph *'Egypt — thou knew'st'* — is an excerpt from a letter (L 430) Dickinson wrote and sent to Susan Huntington Dickinson (about 1874) in *The Letters of Emily Dickinson* (Johnson et al, 1986), p. 533. Dickinson's epigraph quotes Shakespeare's

Antony and Cleopatra in the voice of Antony, with whom Dickinson identified (III, xi, 60): https://www.folger.edu/explore/shakespeares-works/antony-and-cleopatra/read/3/11/#line-3.11.60

"My Cleopatra" includes reference to Atropos, one of the three Greek goddesses, who are also sisters, of fate and destiny. Atropos is the oldest and inflexible goddess of the three and can terminate the lives of mortals by cutting their life threads, the same life threads that her two sisters spin and measure. The nightshade, *Atropa belladonna*, was named by Linnaeus after Atropos because of the toxic properties of the plant when ingested. Its use includes application by drops to dilate pupils and when used by young women for cosmetic purposes was deemed to rouse youthful innocence and to seduce.

In "Arabian Nights, #1," its last stanza, and in "Arabian Nights, #2," its 3rd stanza, the italicized phrase, *the bearded Pronoun*, is borrowed from Dickinson's letter (L 1026) published in *The Letters of Emily Dickinson* (Johnson et al, 1986), p. 894. The meaning of this phrase as it appears in the two poems follows Judith Farr's speculation in her work *The Passion of Emily Dickinson* (1992), p. 176, quoting: "…[S]o customary is Dickinson's association of herself with the vanquished Roman [Antony] that she reserves to herself 'the bearded Pronoun.'"

In "Dear Divers, *my Fellow Men* —," the word "Divers" is borrowed from Dickinson's poem 84 and proposed by Judith Farr to be Dickinson's "code word" in singular for "man." The poem's title in its salutation also borrows and repeats italicized words, "my Fellow Men," as they appear in the 1st epigraph from Dickinson's poem, 1640. Italicized text in the 4th stanza identifies a phrase from Jay Leyda's "Introduction" to his work, *The Years and Hours of Emily Dickinson* (New Haven, Yale University Press, 1960). *Leontodon* is the name of a plant genus, known in English medieval times as "hawkbits" from the belief that when hawks ate the plant, it improved their eyesight, hence, this poem uses this added meaning in its phrase "See me?"

"*Susan's Calls are like Antony's Supper* —" is a poem title borrowed from its epigraph excerpted from a letter (L 854) Dickinson wrote and sent to Susan Huntington Dickinson in spring 1883 in *The Letters of Emily Dickinson* (Johnson et al, eds.,1986), p. 791. This epigraph also includes from this same letter, Dickinson's variation of a quote from Shakespeare's *Antony and Cleopatra* (Enobarbus, II, ii, 264-5): https://www.folger.edu/explore/shakespeares-works/antony-and-cleopatra/read/2/2/?#line-2.2.264. Italicized text in the 3rd stanza is an adaptation of Shakespeare's quote.

In "*Paire de corps*," the poem's title, which reappears in the text as italicized, is a 16th C. French phrase referring to a "pair of bodies," named for a two-piece corset. By the 17th C., these "bodies" became known as "stays," which were stiffened by baleen or whale bones.

In "Clothesline," the word "Cimmerian" is taken from Classical Mythology and refers to a northern people, who live in perpetual darkness.

In "Jasminum," *Ninlil* was a Sumerian goddess of wind, air, and breath, who was also revered as the goddess of destiny. This poem includes references to two types of jasmine known as *Poet's Jasmine* and *White Arabian*. "Queen of the Night" is a name ascribed in India to the night-blooming plant. The word "animalic" refers to the making of perfume when animal products are used to enhance the particular fragrance of musk.

In "Arcturus," *Enlil*, a major Mesopotamian god and husband of *Ninlil*, was the "mooring-rope" connecting heaven and earth, which he had separated so seeds could grow between them in the crevice he created. To break the earth's crust, *Enlil* invented the hoe. He was also recognized as the Sumerian god of agriculture among several other primary functions and elements.

"Today, I go fugitive," references an experience by a dying mother as described in Camille Norton's poem, "Telling the Bees."

In "Limning, Death," the word "Limning" draws its meaning from its Latin root "luminare," which means to give light. The process of "limning" in art refers to an artist's outlining or delineating a subject or object by pencil or brush, a meaning this poem also uses. An "impalement artist," a phrase that appears in this poem, is associated with a spinning human target, usually a female called "target girl." She is pinned to a circular board at the mercy of a knife thrower in a circus stunt referred to as "The Wheel of Death."

"The *Loaded Gun* (Translations No. 1, 2, and 3)," inspired by Dickinson's poem, "*My Life had stood — a Loaded Gun —*" (754), borrow in their titles the italicized words "*Loaded Gun*" as these words appear in Dickinson's poem title, i.e. the first line of her poem. These three poetic "Translations" render different responses as originally conceived and crafted by this author in conversation with Dickinson's I-speaker in her controversial poem (754), which, otherwise, refuses consensus and defies universal meaning. In "Translation No. 3," the italicized text in its last stanza echoes Dickinson's I-speaker and represents one of this author's interpretations of Dickinson's last stanza.

ACKNOWLEDGMENTS

Thank you to the editors of the following journals in which these poems are forthcoming, have appeared, or otherwise acknowledged, sometimes in different versions:

Broad River Review: "The Victorian Dissident" (finalist for the 2022 Rash Award for poetry) in the Fall 2022 issue, Volume 54.

California Quarterly: "Far Reach;" "Bedchamber with Bright's;" and "*Susan's Calls are like Antony's Supper* —" in the 2024 Summer Issue, Volume 50 Number 2.

Catamaran: "The Daguerreotype [camera obscura]" (winner of The Morton Marcus Memorial Poetry Prize 2023) in the Winter Issue 2023.

Cloudbank: "Dear Sir, (No. 3)" in the 2024 Issue No. 18.

Connecticut River Review: "Dents de Lion" (second place prize winner for The Vivian Shipley Poetry Award 2022) in the 2023 Issue.

Crosswinds Poetry Journal: "Limning, Death" in the Spring 2024 Contest Edition.

Emily Dickinson International Society Bulletin: "Sparrow's Sonnet;" "Poiesis;" and "In the bedlam of my chest" in the 2024 May/June Issue, Vol. 36, No. 1.

Five Points: "For Eve at the Evergreens" and "Transitus," Vol. 22, Issue No. 1.

New South: "Arabian Nights, #1" (published as "Arabian Nights, #2"), Vol. 15, Issue 2.

Nimrod International Journal: "Dear Sir (No. 7)" (semifinalist for the Pablo Neruda Prize in Poetry) (published as "Dear Master, No. 7)" in the Awards Issue, fall 2022.

phoebe: "French Sardines" (finalist for the Spring Contest 2023) in the Spring 2023 Issue 52.2.

Reed Magazine: "Arcturus" in Issue 156, Spring 2023.

RHINO Poetry: "Foxglove [disambiguation]" (finalist for the Founders' Prize) in the 2023 Issue.

River Heron Review: "Kiting April" (runner-up for the 2023 River Heron Poetry Prize) in the 2023 August Issue 6.2.

Southword: New International Writing: "The *Loaded Gun* (Translation No. 3)" as "The Loaded Gun in Translation" (finalist for the 2023 Gregory O'Donoghue International Poetry Competition, The Munster Literature Centre, Cork, Ireland) in the 2024 Summer Issue 46.

Suisun Valley Review: "Gentian;" "Jasminum;" "My Voyage;" "Arabian Nights, #2" (as "Arabian Nights, #1"); "The Last Fall;" "Today, I go fugitive —;" and "Dear Sir, (No. 6)" (featured poems) in the Spring 2024, Issue 40.

Sunspot Literary Journal: "Dear Susan, I Am Your Antony — Emily D." (named "Best of Poetry" and runner-up for the 2024 Geminga Prize) in the 2024 digital quarterly edition and in the 2024 annual print edition.

The Banyan Review: "My Windows" (semi-finalist for the 2023 Banyan Poetry Prize) in the 2023 Fall Awards Issue 16.

The Telluride Institute Talking Gourds: "Clothesline" (finalist for the 25th Annual Fischer Prize, appeared online, the 2022 Fischer/Cantor Prize Winning Poems) in the October 2022 Issue.

Third Coast: "*Paire de corps*" in the 2024 Spring Issue 53.

Tupelo Press: "Dear Sir (No. 4)" quoted in its online announcement of "The Results of the Summer Open Reading Period," November 2022.

"French Sardines;" "The Daguerreotype [camera obscura];" "*Paire de corps*;" and "Limning, Death" selected as finalist for a 2024 Maine Literary Award, Short Works Competition in Poetry.

"*Paire de corps*;" "Dear Divers, *my Fellow Men*;" and "The *Loaded Gun* (Translation No. 2)" selected as finalist for the 2024 Pinch Literary Awards in Poetry.

"Othered [I speak]" (as "What the Othered Can't Have"); "*Paire de corps*;" "Dear Divers, *my Fellow Men*;" "*Susan's Calls are like Antony's Supper* —;" and "Dear Sir, (No. 3)" selected as finalist for *CutBank*'s 2024 Patricia Goedicke Prize in Poetry.

"For Eve at the Evergreens;" "Gentian;" "Arabian Nights, #1 (as "My Arabian Nights, #2"); "Dear Sir, (No. 3);" and "Arcturus" selected as finalist submission for the 2022 *New Letters'* Patricia Cleary Miller Prize for Poetry.

"Arcturus" short-listed for the 2022 River Heron Poetry Prize.

"Gentian;" "*Susan's Calls are like Antony's Supper* —" (as "*My Heart Pays for What My Eyes Eat*"); "My Voyage;" and "Dear Divers, *my Fellow Men*" selected as finalist submission for the Grist 2022 ProForma Contest.

"The Last Fall" selected as a finalist for a 2022 Maine Literary Award, Short Works Competition in Poetry.

"Foxglove [disambiguation]" long-listed for the 2023 *Australian Book Review's* Peter Porter Poetry Prize.

"The *Loaded Gun* (Translation #3)," version 1, selected as finalist for the *Quarterly West's* 2022 Annual Poetry Contest, appeared in 2023 Issue 108.

"*Paire de corps*" longlisted for the *Room Magazine* 2023 Poetry Contest.

Called Back, manuscript, one of two finalists for the 2022 May Sarton New Hampshire Poetry Prize and finalist for the 2022 Cider Press Review Editor's Prize.

First and foremost, *Called Back* is a eulogistic celebration of Emily Dickinson and her radical brilliance and passion. *Called Back* owes its initial inspiration and imagination to *Open Me Carefully, Emily Dickinson's Intimate Letters to Susan Huntington Dickinson*, co-edited by Ellen Louise Hart and Martha Nell Smith. As *Called Back* traversed stages of its ontogeny, none of it would have been possible without the midwifery of Stephen Haven, my poet companion, and Catherine Frances, my spouse. Their belief in this work kept my midnight lamps burning and for them I have infinite appreciation in the making of *Called Back* from start to finish. I am grateful to Ruth Hughes, poet and friend, for her assistance and education on historical language and words that carry into current time negative implications of racism. As a result of Ruth's guidance, *Called Back*, "For the othered," is hopeful in its strive toward a language that is culturally and socio-politically sensitive. Savored for the last is my gratitude to Jeffrey Levine, Publisher; Kristina Marie Darling, Editor in Chief; and Cassandra Cleghorn, Poetry Editor at Tupelo Press for selecting *Called Back* during Tupelo's 2022 Summer Open Reading Period. Especially,

Jeffrey's masterful eye at the editing phase of publication was brilliant and sheer magic. I am indebted to Kristina Marie Darling; David Rossitter, Managing Editor; Allison O'Keefe, Designer; and Tupelo's support staff for their unending assistance in ushering *Called Back* into the world. The team at Tupelo Press is topnotch, and I am thankful and proud to be one of its authors and a recipient of such support from one of the best publishers of literary import. Thank you, Tupelo, and all those who have made this work possible.